THE BIRTH OF JESUS

Adapted by
Etta G. Wilson

Illustrations by
Thomas Gianni

Publications International, Ltd.

In the town of Nazareth lived a young woman named Mary. She was engaged to marry a carpenter named Joseph. Mary would often stop in the doorway of Joseph's shop to say hello.

Long before they met, one of God's prophets had said, "An unmarried woman will have a baby boy, and his name will mean that God is with us."

One day, God sent an angel to Mary. The angel said, "God is pleased with you, Mary. You will have a son and you must name him Jesus. He will be called the Son of God. He will have a kingdom that will never end."

Mary asked, "How can this happen? I'm not married."

Gabriel answered her, "Nothing is impossible for God."

"I want to please God," Mary said. "If this is what God wants, then let it be."

Joseph was upset to learn that Mary was going to have a baby. He decided to call off their marriage.

One night while Joseph was asleep, an angel from God spoke to him in a dream. The angel explained to Joseph that Mary's baby was from God's Holy Spirit.

When Joseph woke up, he went to see Mary. He told her what the angel had said. They were married soon after that.

At about this same time, the emperor decided to count all the people living in his country for the tax records. Everyone had to go to their home town to be counted. Joseph and Mary started off to Bethlehem, the home town of Joseph's family.

The trip was very hard, especially for Mary, because it was almost time for the baby to come. As they came into the town, they could see it was already crowded.

Joseph tried to get a room for the night, but the inns were all full. Finally, he took Mary to a stable because there was no other place to stay. There, she gave birth to her baby. She and Joseph named him Jesus, just as the angels had told them.

Mary wrapped her new baby in wide strips of cloth she had brought from home. She laid Jesus in an empty manger, a place where the animals ate. Joseph and Mary were very happy.

That same night, some shepherds were guarding their sheep near Bethlehem. All at once, they saw an angel from God in the sky.

The angel said, "Don't be afraid. I'm bringing you wonderful news. Tonight a Savior was born for you and your people. He is Jesus the Lord. Go and see him. You will find him in a stable, lying in a manger."

Suddenly the sky was full of angels singing praises to God.

ተ፯

After the angels left, the shepherds were very excited. They went straight to Bethlehem to look for the new baby. They told everyone they met what the angel had said out in the fields. They found Jesus in the stable with Mary and Joseph, and they looked at the little baby in wonder.

Later, the shepherds went back to their sheep, singing thanks to God for the new baby. Everything they had heard and seen was just as the angel had told them.

A little later, some wise men who studied the stars came from a land far to the east. They had followed a special bright star to Jerusalem.

"Where is the baby who was born to be your king?" they asked. "We followed his special star from the east and we want to worship him."

The wise men learned that Jesus was to be born in Bethlehem. So they left for that town, following the bright star all the way.

ተተ

The star stopped right over the place where Joseph, Mary, and the baby were staying. The wise men went in and knelt down to worship the new baby. They gave him special gifts.

Later, an angel warned Joseph that the king of the land was afraid of Jesus and wanted to kill the little baby. To be safe, Joseph took his family to Egypt. When the king died, they returned to Nazareth, where Jesus grew strong and wise, and pleased God in everything he did.

ተየ